Handbook on Profiles of Indian Financial Institutions

Battula Vijay Kiran

M.Tech., M.B.A., Ph.D.

Prof. A. Narasimha Rao

M.Com., M.B.A., Ph.D., FCMA
DCMS, College of Arts and Commerce, Andhra University

NOTION PRESS

NOTION PRESS

India. Singapore. Malaysia.

ISBN 979-8896730187 (Paper Back)
ISBN 979-8896730194 (Hard Cover)

Contents

Preface

India's financial system is vast, diverse, and often difficult to understand because of the large number of institutions, regulators, intermediaries, and specialised entities that operate within it. Information about these organisations is frequently scattered across reports, websites, statutes, and regulatory publications, making it challenging for students, researchers, professionals, and general readers to develop a clear overall picture.

This handbook was prepared to provide a structured overview of the major institutions that form India's financial architecture. The chapters are organised broadly according to the regulatory framework governing these entities, covering institutions associated with the Reserve Bank of India, public financial institutions, securities markets, insurance, corporate affairs, pensions, and other important segments of the financial system.

The objective of this handbook is simple: to help readers identify key institutions, understand their primary functions, and appreciate how they fit within the broader financial ecosystem. It is intended as a convenient reference for students, competitive examination aspirants, researchers, professionals, and anyone interested in understanding the institutional framework of India's financial system.

Note to Readers: This handbook is an honest effort by the author to bring together information on Indian financial institutions in a single, structured volume after observing a gap in the available literature during the course of academic research. **The information presented in this book has been compiled, reviewed, and updated up to late 2024.** While every reasonable effort has been made to ensure accuracy and reliability, **this book**

may still contain inadvertent errors, omissions, outdated information, inconsistencies, or differing interpretations that may have escaped the author's attention despite thorough review.

Readers are strongly encouraged not to treat every statement in this handbook as an unquestionable or final authority. Instead, this book should be viewed as a **foundational and directional guide** that helps readers understand the structure, roles, and relationships of India's financial institutions. The real benefit of this handbook lies in providing a consolidated starting point from which readers can explore the subject in greater depth.

After completing the book, readers are sincerely encouraged to re-examine and verify important facts, figures, institutional details, regulations, and interpretations using official publications, regulatory notifications, annual reports, statutes, circulars, and institutional websites. Such independent verification will not only help identify any inaccuracies that may remain but will also significantly enhance the reader's knowledge and understanding beyond what any single handbook can provide. The idea for this work originated solely from the author after identifying a need for such a handbook during academic research. **The supervising professor's contribution was limited to guidance on general academic writing and textbook preparation. The selection of content, compilation of information, interpretations presented, and any errors or omissions that may remain are solely the responsibility of the author and should not be attributed to the supervising professor.**

Battula Vijay Kiran

Acknowledgments

A book of this kind is never the work of one person alone, and it is a pleasure to record my debts here.

My first thanks go to Prof. A. Narasimha Rao, M.Com., M.B.A., Ph.D., FCMA, who joined this project as co-author while serving as Research Director and Principal of the College of Arts and Commerce. His encouragement was steady, his reading was careful, and his judgment shaped the book at every turn. Working with him has been a genuine education.

Above all, I thank my parents, Sri B. Sivanandam and Smt. Bhavani, for their love and their belief in me, which carried this work to its end. My siblings and relatives gave me strength of their own kind, and I am thankful for it.

Battula Vijay Kiran

CHAPTER 1

Introduction to the Indian Financial System

The Indian financial system is the framework through which money moves between the people and bodies that have it and those that need it: households, firms, governments, and participants from abroad. It is built from institutions, markets, instruments, services, and regulators, and its task is to gather savings and direct them to productive use. The system has grown over decades to keep pace with a widening economy and a varied population, and as India reaches for faster growth, deeper global ties, and a more inclusive economy, the financial system remains the engine that carries those ambitions forward.

Before classifying institutions and markets in detail, it helps to be clear about what the system is for. This opening chapter therefore stays at the level of purpose and design. It sets out the work the financial system performs and the goals it serves, so that the institution profiles in the chapters that follow have a frame to sit within.

1.1 What the Financial System Does

At its most basic, the financial system turns idle savings into working capital. Households and firms with money to spare place it in banks, non-banking financial companies, mutual funds, insurance products, and other channels. Those pooled funds are then lent or invested in the businesses, infrastructure, and public programmes that need capital to grow and to create jobs. Without such a mechanism, money would sit unused or move clumsily, and economic development would stall. Directing savings to their most productive uses is the first and most important function the system performs.

A second function is the settlement of payments. Modern commerce depends on money changing hands safely and on time, and the financial system supplies the means, from the distribution of physical currency to electronic transfers, mobile banking, and the digital rails that now carry most retail payments. When people and firms trust that a payment will clear quickly and without loss, trade flows more freely and confidence in the wider economy holds.

The system also helps participants manage risk. Economic life is full of uncertainty, from the chance that a borrower defaults to swings in interest rates, currencies, and markets. Insurance policies, futures, options, credit derivatives, and diversified portfolios all give firms and households ways to guard against loss. Banks weigh the creditworthiness of borrowers, insurers spread risk across many policyholders, and markets price securities according to the risks they carry, and together these practices make the environment steadier for everyone in it.

Finally, the system discovers prices. By bringing buyers, sellers, and intermediaries together in regulated markets, it settles on the value of financial instruments. A share price on a stock exchange reflects the balance struck between those who want to buy and those who want to sell, and so signals what the market thinks a company is worth. Bond yields, in the same way, reveal how investors judge the creditworthiness of an issuer. These signals guide where capital flows and reward firms that are well run.

1.2 What the System Aims to Achieve

Beyond these everyday functions, the financial system is built around a few broad goals. The first is stability. Bank failures, market crashes, and systemic crises destroy public confidence and damage the real economy, so the Reserve Bank of India and the other regulators work to keep institutions well capitalised, to hold credit growth within safe limits, and to stop markets from running into speculative excess. Stress tests, prudential rules, and close supervision together build a system that can absorb shocks at home and from abroad.

The second goal is inclusion. India's population is vast and unevenly served, and a financial system that reaches only the cities or the well-off leaves most of the country behind. Inclusion means putting basic banking, affordable credit, insurance, and a place to save within reach of rural households, low-income families, and small firms. Microfinance institutions, payment banks, and digital services have brought many more people into the formal system, and in doing so have narrowed old inequalities.

The third goal pairs efficiency with transparency. An efficient system keeps the cost of connecting savers and borrowers low, which can mean cheaper credit, better returns on savings, and higher productivity overall. Transparency earns the trust that makes the rest possible. Savers, investors, and policyholders need accurate and timely information about the products they buy, the firms they deal with, and the rules that govern them, and clear disclosure backed by firm enforcement is what gives them confidence to take part.

1.3 Classification of the Indian Financial System

The system can be read along three lines: the institutions that hold and move money, the markets in which instruments are traded, and the services that support both. The sections below take each in turn.

1.3.1 Institutions

Institutions are the main channels through which funds pass from savers to borrowers, and through which businesses, households, and the government obtain financial services. Each type carries its own function, its own rules, and its own place in the market.

Banks

Banks sit at the centre of the system. They take deposits, extend credit, and run the payment and settlement services on which daily commerce depends. Commercial banks are the largest and most influential group. They include the public sector banks owned by the government, such as the State Bank of India, alongside private banks that may be Indian or foreign owned. Their customers range from large corporations and government agencies to small firms and ordinary savers, and their products span savings and current accounts, fixed deposits, personal and business loans, trade finance, and foreign exchange. Operating under the supervision of the RBI, commercial banks carry monetary policy through to the wider economy and help keep credit flowing.

Cooperative banks are set up under cooperative law and run on the principle of mutual help and member control. Owned and managed by their members, they serve both towns and villages, and they tend to concentrate on the credit needs of small borrowers, farmers, and local businesses. Because they are at once cooperative societies and financial institutions, they answer both to the RBI and to the state or central cooperative authorities.

Regional rural banks were created to carry credit and banking to rural and semi-urban areas, and so to support agriculture, small industry, and the activities that depend on them. Established by statute and sponsored by larger commercial banks, they extend services to regions that mainstream banking has often passed over, and they remain important to the rural economy.

Non-Banking Financial Companies

Non-banking financial companies, or NBFCs, offer many of the same services as banks, including loans, leasing, hire purchase, and investment products, but they hold no banking licence. They cannot accept demand deposits, and they raise funds instead through debentures, equity, and other market instruments. NBFCs tend to serve niches that banks reach less easily, among them microfinance, vehicle finance, infrastructure lending, and consumer credit. Regulated chiefly by the RBI, and in some cases by other authorities according to what they do, they widen the financial system, sharpen competition, and bring credit to borrowers the banks might miss.

Insurance Companies

Insurance companies protect against risk by pooling premiums from many policyholders and paying out to those who suffer a covered loss, whether to life, health, property, or liability. The sector divides into life insurers, general insurers covering health, motor, and property, and specialised insurers handling lines such as crop cover and reinsurance. Regulated by the Insurance Regulatory and Development Authority of India, insurers encourage long-term saving, invest large sums in the capital markets, and steady the wider economy by spreading risk.

Pension Funds

Pension funds collect contributions from workers and employers across a working life and return them as income after retirement.

Some are public bodies, such as the Employees' Provident Fund Organisation, while others are private providers. They invest these long-term savings in government securities, corporate bonds, and equities, supplying steady capital to the economy while securing an income for the retired. The Pension Fund Regulatory and Development Authority oversees much of this work, holding providers to prudent investment and adequate coverage.

Other Intermediaries

Several further intermediaries perform specialised tasks. Mutual funds, managed by asset management companies, pool money from many investors and place it across a diversified portfolio, opening equity, debt, and money markets to people who lack the capital or expertise to enter them alone. Merchant bankers and investment banks help companies raise capital, advise on mergers and acquisitions, and manage public offerings. Credit rating agencies judge the creditworthiness of borrowers and their instruments, giving investors a measure of the risk involved. Venture capital firms and private equity funds back start-ups and growing companies, supplying not only money but guidance, and so encourage innovation and enterprise. Specialised and development finance institutions concentrate on particular sectors, such as agriculture, small industry, foreign trade, housing, or infrastructure, and provide credit and advice tailored to them.

Taken together, these institutions act as complementary pillars. Each brings its own strengths, and between them they make sure that firms, individuals, and every segment of society can find suitable financial services. By spreading risk, allocating capital well, and supporting new ideas, they hold up India's growth and stability.

1.3.2 Markets

Markets are the arenas in which financial instruments are bought, sold, priced, and traded, from overnight loans to long-dated equity. They let participants raise capital, manage liquidity, hedge risk, and invest savings, and they perform the work of price discovery by drawing many buyers and sellers together. Different markets suit different time horizons and different appetites for risk.

The Money Market

The money market handles short-term funds, with maturities running from overnight to a year. It gives banks, NBFCs, and companies a place to manage their daily cash, and it trades in a handful of well-defined instruments. Treasury bills are short-term securities issued by the central government to meet immediate funding needs; treated as virtually risk-free, they set the benchmark for other short-term rates. Commercial paper consists of unsecured promissory notes issued by highly rated companies to fund working capital, offering more return than treasury bills at somewhat greater risk. Certificates of deposit are negotiable short-term deposits issued by banks, letting them raise funds while giving investors a safe, interest-bearing place to park money. Call and notice money refers to very short loans, often overnight or up to a fortnight, used among banks to balance their daily liquidity. By keeping short-term funds moving, the money market steadies the banking system, shapes interest rates, and helps the central bank carry out monetary policy.

The Capital Market

The capital market deals in medium and long-term finance, and it has two main parts. In the equity market, companies raise capital by issuing shares to the public, and those who buy them become part-owners entitled to a share of profits and any rise in value. The Bombay Stock Exchange and the National Stock Exchange handle most of this trading, and the market rewards good governance, since listed companies answer to their shareholders, while continuously discovering the price that reflects a company's prospects. In the debt market, issuers sell bonds and debentures, promising to repay the principal with interest over time. This suits investors who prefer steadier returns and less volatility than shares carry. Government bonds, considered low in risk, fund public spending, while corporate bonds pay more but carry more risk. A well-functioning debt market gives infrastructure projects and corporate expansion a stable source of long-term finance. The Securities and Exchange Board of India regulates the capital market, and by enforcing disclosure and protecting investors it keeps the market sound and confidence intact.

The Foreign Exchange Market

The foreign exchange market is where currencies are traded. It is a global market in which banks, financial institutions, companies, and individuals buy and sell currencies to settle international trade, invest abroad, manage their exposure, or take a position on currency movements. For India, it underpins cross-border business and helps the RBI keep the exchange rate stable. In the spot market, currencies change hands for immediate delivery, while the forward market uses contracts that fix a rate for settlement at a future date, allowing firms to hedge against adverse swings. The RBI steps into the market to curb volatility, build reserves, and hold the exchange rate steady, and a well-managed market here reduces currency risk and reassures foreign investors.

The Derivatives Market

Derivatives are instruments whose value comes from an underlying asset, such as a stock, bond, commodity, currency, or index. They let investors manage price risk, take a view on future movements, or lock in a price ahead of time. Futures bind buyer and seller to trade an asset at a set price and date, while options give the holder the right, though not the obligation, to buy or sell at a fixed price, and both are widely used to hedge against adverse moves in equities, commodities, and currencies. Swaps let institutions exchange cash flows to manage interest rate or currency risk, and forwards are customised over-the-counter contracts that trade flexibility for the standardisation of futures. The derivatives market adds depth to the system. It can introduce complexity and risk of its own, but strict rules on disclosure, margin, and clearing keep it a tool for managing risk rather than a source of instability.

1.3.3 Services

Around the institutions and markets sits a layer of services that make the whole system work more smoothly. They speed up transactions, lower costs, improve transparency, and help participants manage risk, and they apply equally to individuals, companies, and the government.

Payment and Settlement Services

Payment and settlement services are the backbone of the system, moving funds between parties safely and on time. They run from older instruments such as cheques and demand drafts to online banking, mobile wallets, and transactions on the Unified Payments Interface. Digital networks and banking apps have cut the time and cost of payments sharply, which matters most for reaching parts of the country that conventional banking long overlooked. Behind these payments, bodies such as the National Payments Corporation of India and the Clearing Corporation of India Ltd. clear and settle payment instruments and securities trades, reducing counterparty risk and giving payments their finality.

Credit Rating Services

Credit rating agencies assess how creditworthy a borrower is, whether a company, a government, or a financial institution, and rate the debt it issues. By weighing financial health, debt levels, business risk, and governance, they give investors a clear measure of risk. A high rating points to lower credit risk, a low one warns of possible default, and so ratings help investors match instruments to the risk they are willing to bear. The presence of credible ratings also presses issuers to keep their finances in order, which lowers the cost of capital for those that do.

Merchant Banking and Advisory Services

Merchant bankers and investment bankers help companies raise capital and advise them through mergers, acquisitions, public offerings, and private placements. They guide issuers through a thicket of regulation, structure the instruments to be sold, and connect them with investors, and by underwriting issues they smooth the path of funds from the market into productive use. Beyond raising money, they advise on growth strategy, the restructuring of balance sheets, the valuation of targets, and relations with investors, all of which sharpens how efficiently companies operate.

Brokerage, Custodial, and Depository Services

A further set of services lets participants trade, hold, and manage their assets securely. Stockbrokers stand between buyers and sellers in the equity and debt markets, providing the platforms, research, and execution that investors rely on. Custodians safeguard securities and other assets for institutional and retail investors, handling dividends, interest, and corporate actions on their behalf. Depositories, in India the National Securities Depository Limited and the Central Depository Services Limited, hold ownership records in electronic form. By doing away with paper certificates, they have cut operational risk, transaction costs, and settlement times, and they have made the market both safer and more transparent.

Leasing and Factoring

Leasing and factoring offer firms ways to fund themselves outside the usual channels. A leasing company lets a business use equipment, machinery, or vehicles for a fixed term in return for periodic payments, which conserves capital and keeps the firm flexible. A factoring firm buys a company's receivables at a discount and pays cash at once, freeing up working capital and shifting the burden of collection off the firm.

Venture Capital and Private Equity

Venture capital and private equity funds back companies with strong growth prospects that cannot easily raise money the conventional way. Venture capital firms support start-ups and early-stage companies, accepting high risk for the chance of high return, and they often bring mentoring and contacts alongside their money. Private equity funds invest in more mature companies, frequently taking large stakes to steer strategy, lift operating performance, and ready the firm for a sale or a listing. Between them they help sectors as varied as manufacturing, technology, and consumer goods to grow.

1.4 The Overall Structure of Financial Institutions in India

1.4.1 All India Financial Institutions

All India Financial Institutions support the country's long-term development by supplying finance that ordinary banking does not fully provide. Backed by the government and regulated by the RBI and other statutory bodies, they concentrate on strategic sectors and developmental aims, and their work complements that of commercial banks by steering credit to parts of the economy that matter for balanced growth.

Development Banks

Development banks were set up to provide medium and long-term credit to sectors judged vital to progress, such as industry, infrastructure, agriculture, and small enterprise. Unlike commercial banks, which lean toward short-term lending and deposit taking, they finance projects with long horizons and high social returns. In industrial finance, institutions such as the former Industrial Development Bank of India and the Industrial Finance Corporation of India funded large industries and supported the country's early industrialisation; although some have since merged or changed form, their place in India's industrial history is secure. Development banks also lend for infrastructure, including roads, railways, power, and ports, and for rural projects such as irrigation, electrification, and farm storage, the investments on which broader growth rests.

Specialised Financial Institutions

Specialised institutions serve particular parts of the economy, offering finance and advice shaped to a niche and filling gaps that mainstream banking leaves open. In trade, the Export-Import

Bank of India supports international commerce with export credit, guarantees, and insurance, helping Indian firms reach foreign markets and manage the risks of cross-border business. Other specialised bodies direct credit and expertise to priority areas such as housing, small and medium enterprises, and agriculture, so that growth extends into rural communities, low-income groups, and emerging industries that lack easy access to credit.

Investment Institutions

Investment institutions channel both retail and institutional money into productive assets and so add to capital formation. Many have since diversified or merged into the wider financial sector, but their influence remains. Public investment institutions once underwrote industrial ventures, bought shares and bonds, and took part in the capital markets to support corporate expansion, and in doing so they helped private investment and enterprise take root. By placing funds in equity and debt, they deepened India's capital markets, improved liquidity, and strengthened the discovery of prices, to the benefit of investors and issuers alike.

Refinance Institutions

Refinance institutions lend not to final borrowers but to other intermediaries, among them banks, NBFCs, and microfinance institutions, and so multiply their reach by working through existing networks. In agriculture and rural credit, the National Bank for Agriculture and Rural Development refinances rural cooperative banks, regional rural banks, and other rural lenders, strengthening the rural credit system and helping farmers obtain seasonal credit and invest in better methods. Similar support flows to housing finance companies and infrastructure lenders, keeping credit moving to affordable housing and to projects that improve connectivity, energy, and urban life.

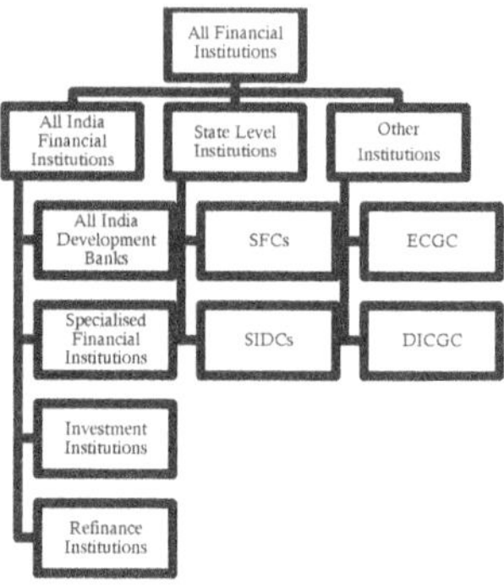

Source: Reserve Bank of India

Figure 1. Classification of Financial Institutions in India

1.4.2 State Level Institutions

Alongside the all-India bodies, India has institutions that work at the level of the state. They were created to direct finance, promote industry, and develop the economy within their own borders, and by tying credit to regional priorities they address local imbalances, support small and medium enterprises, and contribute to more even growth across the country.

State Financial Corporations

State Financial Corporations are government-sponsored bodies set up under the State Financial Corporations Act, and their task is to finance small and medium industry within a state. They provide term loans, working capital, and other credit to firms that mainstream commercial banking often overlooks, especially start-ups and businesses in less-developed areas. By directing long-term finance to manufacturing, agro-based units, and service enterprises, they support ventures that create local jobs, and because they work close to the ground, they can fit their lending to the particular conditions of a state and so narrow the gap between cities and the regions around them.

State Industrial Development Corporations

State Industrial Development Corporations were formed to build industrial infrastructure and draw investment into particular states. Their roles vary, but they commonly acquire and develop land for industrial estates, offer financial and technical help to new ventures, and bring together government, private investors, and financial institutions. They lay out estates, parks, and zones with roads, power, and water, which lowers the barriers to entry and encourages industry to spread beyond the established centres. Beyond finance, they often assist with licensing, approvals, and compliance, and they support technology upgrades, skill development, and marketing, all of which lift the competitiveness of industry within the state.

1.4.3 Other Institutions

A few further institutions exist mainly to protect the integrity of the system, to contain risk, and to keep confidence steady. Two stand out.

Export Credit Guarantee Corporation

The Export Credit Guarantee Corporation of India Limited is a government-owned body that strengthens India's export trade by insuring and guaranteeing against the risks of selling abroad. By covering exporters against losses from buyer default, political upheaval, or currency swings, it gives them the confidence to enter unfamiliar markets. Its guarantees also make banks more willing to fund exporters, since loans backed by the corporation carry less risk, and with that backing exporters, including small and medium firms, can diversify into new geographies, widen their customer base, and add to the country's foreign exchange earnings.

Deposit Insurance and Credit Guarantee Corporation

The Deposit Insurance and Credit Guarantee Corporation protects depositors by insuring the deposits they hold in banks, and its purpose is to keep public confidence in banking intact. If an insured bank fails, depositors are repaid up to a set limit, and that assurance keeps small savers within the formal system rather than outside it. By making bank runs and panic withdrawals less likely in times of stress, deposit insurance reinforces trust in banking, and a banking system that holds public trust is far less prone to the crises that disrupt the wider economy.

1.4.4 How Non-Banking Financial Companies Are Regulated

Non-banking financial companies provide many of the services that banks do, including lending, investment, and advice, yet they differ in important ways. They hold no banking licence, cannot accept demand deposits, and tend to specialise more narrowly. Even so, they deepen the financial system, widen access to credit, and bring fresh approaches to financial services. They register under the Companies Act, 2013, which replaced the older Companies Act of 1956, and depending on what they do, they fall under the supervision of different regulators, so that each kind meets prudential standards suited to its work.

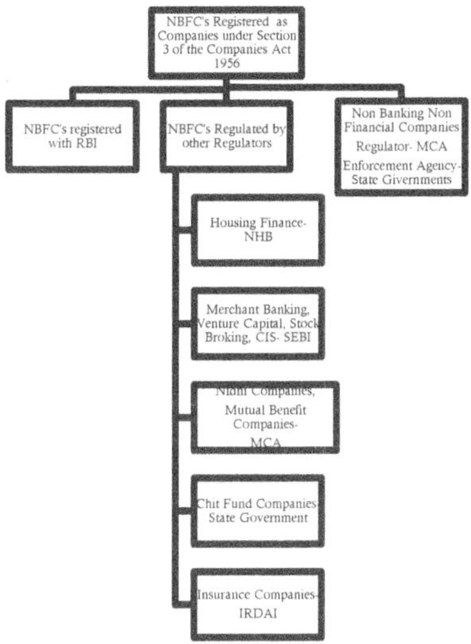

Source: Reserve Bank of India

Figure 2. Regulation of NBFCs

Many NBFCs come under the direct supervision of the RBI. These may carry out lending, asset finance, hire purchase, leasing, and factoring, and the central bank sets their norms for capital adequacy, asset classification, provisioning, and governance. Its oversight is meant to protect financial stability and the soundness of the companies within its charge.

Not every NBFC answers to the RBI alone. Some perform specialised functions that place them under other authorities. Housing finance companies, which lend for home purchase, construction, and real estate, are regulated by the Reserve Bank of India, which since August 2019 has taken over their regulation from the National Housing Bank; the National Housing Bank continues to refinance and supervise the sector and to keep housing credit well allocated and borrowers protected. Merchant bankers, venture capital funds, stockbrokers, and operators of collective investment schemes come under the SEBI, which enforces disclosure and fair dealing to protect the integrity of the securities markets. Nidhi companies and mutual benefit companies, which encourage thrift and mutual support among their members, are registered under the Companies Act and overseen by the Ministry of Corporate Affairs; they fall outside the RBI's definition of an NBFC and function more as close-knit savings communities. Chit funds, which pool contributions and periodically auction the pool to a member, are regulated by the states through their Registrars of Chits, and although they can meet genuine funding needs, they require firm regulation to guard members against misuse. Insurance companies, though registered under the Companies Act, are regulated chiefly by the IRDAI, which sets solvency standards, product rules, and consumer protections to keep insurers sound and fair.

There are also companies registered under the Companies Act that carry on no financial activity at all and therefore are not NBFCs. These come under the MCA and, in some cases, state authorities. They pursue industrial, commercial, or service activities and do not need the specialised oversight that financial regulators provide.

1.5 The Principal Regulators

Five authorities do most of the regulating in India's financial system, and a short account of each closes this chapter.

The **RBI** is the central bank. It frames and carries out monetary policy, supervises commercial banks and selected NBFCs, manages the country's foreign exchange, and works to keep the financial system stable. It also advances financial inclusion, supports the payment systems, and encourages new approaches in banking.

The **SEBI** oversees the securities markets, covering equities, bonds, derivatives, and mutual funds. Its central task is to protect investors, hold the market to honest disclosure, and regulate the intermediaries, from exchanges and brokers to merchant bankers, that operate within it.

The **IRDAI** regulates life, general, and reinsurance companies. It works to keep insurers solvent, to protect policyholders, and to hold the industry to fair practice, while encouraging new products, fair pricing, and wider insurance coverage.

The **PFRDA** regulates India's pension sector, including the National Pension System and the Atal Pension Yojana. It registers and supervises pension funds and intermediaries, protects the interests of subscribers, and works to extend old-age income security across the country.

The **MCA** administers company law and the standards of corporate governance. It regulates companies under the Companies Act, secures compliance with the law, and supports transparency and responsible conduct in business.

The chapters that follow profile the institutions that operate under these authorities. By taking each regulator and the bodies it supervises in turn, the book builds a clear picture of their distinct roles and of how, together, they hold up the Indian financial system.

CHAPTER 2

Profiles of Institutions under RBI

The Reserve Bank of India sits at the centre of the country's financial system, and around it stands a family of subsidiaries, funded institutions, schemes, market utilities, and statutory bodies that together keep money, credit, and payments flowing safely. This chapter profiles the Reserve Bank itself and then the bodies that operate under, alongside, or with the support of it, its technology subsidiaries, its research and training institutions, its consumer schemes, the laws it administers, the payment and settlement utilities it oversees, and the entities it regulates.

2.1 Reserve Bank of India (RBI)

The Reserve Bank of India (RBI) is the central bank of the country. It was established on 1 April 1935 under the Reserve Bank of India Act, 1934, and was nationalised in 1949. From a body created mainly to issue currency and manage credit in the colonial economy, it has grown into the institution responsible for monetary policy, financial regulation, currency, foreign-exchange management, and the oversight of the payment system. Its head office is in Mumbai.

2.1.1 Establishment and Evolution

Before 1935 the Indian financial system was served by lightly supervised private banks, with no single authority to issue currency, manage public debt, or act as lender of last resort. The Reserve Bank was created to fill that gap. After independence its mandate widened to support planned economic development and the direction of credit to priority sectors, and the nationalisation of major commercial banks in 1969 further enlarged its role in credit control and financial inclusion.

2.1.2 Organisation and Governance

The Reserve Bank is headed by a Governor, supported by Deputy Governors, and is governed by a Central Board of Directors appointed by the Government of India. Monetary policy is set by the Monetary Policy Committee (MPC), constituted in 2016, which fixes the policy interest rate in line with the inflation target agreed with the Government. The Bank works through specialised departments, including the Department of Regulation (which frames prudential rules for banks and non-banking financial companies), the Financial Markets Regulation Department, the Department of Payment and Settlement Systems, and the Department of Economic and Policy Research.

2.1.3 Core Functions

Monetary Policy

The Reserve Bank formulates and implements monetary policy to control inflation, manage the money supply, and support growth. The MPC sets the policy rate, and the Bank uses a set of instruments to give effect to it:

Repo rate: the rate at which the Reserve Bank lends to banks against government securities; raising it restrains borrowing and inflation, lowering it encourages credit and activity.

Standing Deposit Facility (SDF): introduced in April 2022, the rate at which banks park surplus funds with the Reserve Bank; it now forms the floor of the policy corridor, the role earlier played by the reverse repo rate.

Marginal Standing Facility (MSF): the rate at which banks borrow overnight against approved securities; it forms the ceiling of the corridor.

Cash Reserve Ratio and Statutory Liquidity Ratio: the share of deposits banks must keep as reserves with the Reserve Bank and in prescribed liquid assets.

Open market operations: the purchase and sale of government securities to add or absorb liquidity.

Regulation and Supervision

The Reserve Bank licenses, regulates, and supervises commercial banks, cooperative banks, and non-banking financial companies. It sets prudential norms on capital, asset classification, and liquidity, conducts inspections, and can impose corrective action or penalties on institutions that fall short.

Foreign Exchange Management

The Reserve Bank manages the country's foreign-exchange reserves and administers the Foreign Exchange Management Act (FEMA), through which it regulates cross-border transactions and intervenes in the market to limit excessive volatility in the rupee.

Currency, Payments, and Inclusion

As the sole issuer of currency, the Reserve Bank manages the supply, quality, and security of banknotes (the detailed arrangements for printing and minting are set out in Section 2.2). It oversees the safety and efficiency of the payment and settlement systems (Sections 2.8 and 2.11), promotes financial inclusion so that banking reaches under-served and rural populations, and protects consumers through its ombudsman mechanism and financial-literacy work (Sections 2.5 and 2.7).

2.2 Currency Management, Public Debt, and Deposit Insurance

2.2.1 Printing and Minting of Currency

Responsibility for producing currency is shared between the Government of India and the Reserve Bank:

Government presses: banknotes are printed at the Government-owned presses at Nashik (Maharashtra) and Dewas (Madhya Pradesh), run by the Security Printing and Minting Corporation of India Ltd (SPMCIL), a wholly Government-owned company.

Reserve Bank presses: two further presses, at Mysuru (Karnataka) and Salboni (West Bengal), are run by Bharatiya Reserve Bank Note Mudran Pvt Ltd (BRBNMPL), a wholly owned subsidiary of the Reserve Bank.

Coins: coins are minted by the Government of India at the four India Government Mints, Mumbai, Kolkata, Hyderabad, and Noida, and are issued into circulation only through the Reserve Bank.

2.2.2 Public Debt Management

The Reserve Bank manages the borrowing programme of the Central and State Governments. It issues and services government securities, conducts auctions, and provides Ways and Means Advances to cover temporary mismatches between government receipts and payments. The Special Drawing Facility allows State Governments to draw short-term funds against their holdings of government securities at a concessional rate, ahead of normal advances.

2.2.3 Deposit Insurance and Credit Guarantee Corporation (DICGC)

The Deposit Insurance and Credit Guarantee Corporation (DICGC) is a wholly owned subsidiary of the Reserve Bank, established on 15 July 1978 by merging the Deposit Insurance Corporation (1962) and the Credit Guarantee Corporation of India (1971). It insures deposits held in commercial banks, regional rural banks, and cooperative banks up to ₹5 lakh per depositor, a limit raised from ₹1 lakh with effect from February 2020. If an insured bank fails, depositors are compensated up to this limit, which sustains public confidence in the banking system. The corporation's credit-guarantee function has not operated since 2003; deposit insurance is today its sole activity, even though the historical name is retained.

2.3 Technology and Innovation Subsidiaries

The Reserve Bank operates three wholly owned subsidiaries that build and run the technology, security, and innovation infrastructure of the financial sector.

2.3.1 Reserve Bank Information Technology Pvt Ltd (ReBIT)

Set up in 2016, ReBIT strengthens the information-technology and cybersecurity capabilities of the Reserve Bank and its regulated entities. It audits and assesses IT systems, advises on cyber-security standards, and supports the Reserve Bank's technology projects and its risk-based supervision of banks.

2.3.2 Indian Financial Technology and Allied Services (IFTAS)

A wholly owned subsidiary established in 2015, IFTAS provides the core communication and messaging infrastructure of Indian banking. Its services include the Indian Financial Network (INFINET), the Structured Financial Messaging System (SFMS) that carries RTGS and NEFT instructions, and the Indian Banking Community Cloud (IBCC).

2.3.3 Reserve Bank Innovation Hub (RBIH)

Incorporated in 2021 as a Section 8 (not-for-profit) company and inaugurated in Bengaluru in March 2022, RBIH promotes financial innovation and inclusion. It brings together banks, fintech firms, and start-ups to build digital public infrastructure, its best-known projects being the Unified Lending Interface (ULI), which speeds the flow of authenticated data to lenders, and MuleHunter.AI, which detects money-mule accounts used in fraud.

2.4 Research and Training Institutions

The Reserve Bank funds and supports several institutions devoted to research, education, and capacity-building in banking and finance.

2.4.1 Centre for Advanced Financial Research and Learning (CAFRAL)

Set up by the Reserve Bank in 2011, CAFRAL is a not-for-profit research and learning body. It conducts research in areas such as banking, household finance, and macro finance, runs advanced programmes for senior financial-sector executives, and provides a forum for regulators, bankers, and academics. The Governor of the Reserve Bank chairs its governing council.

2.4.2 Indira Gandhi Institute of Development Research (IGIDR)

Established and funded by the Reserve Bank, IGIDR was registered as a society in 1986 and its campus in Mumbai was inaugurated in 1987. A Deemed University under the University Grants Commission, it carries out multidisciplinary research on development, economics, energy, and the environment, and offers M.Sc. and doctoral programmes that train researchers for academia, government, and industry.

2.4.3 Indian Institute of Bank Management (IIBM)

Established in 1980 and located in Guwahati, IIBM is an autonomous institute sponsored by the Reserve Bank, NABARD, and public-sector banks. It trains banking professionals and conducts research, with a particular focus on the banking needs of the North-Eastern region.

2.4.4 National Institute of Bank Management (NIBM)

Established by the Reserve Bank in 1969 and located in Pune, NIBM is an autonomous apex institution for research, training, and consultancy in bank management. It offers a Post-Graduate Diploma in Management (Banking and Financial Services) and advises banks on operations and strategy.

2.5 Consumer Schemes and Digital Platforms

The Reserve Bank runs a number of schemes and online platforms that serve consumers directly, simplify access to its services, and spread financial awareness.

2.5.1 Integrated Ombudsman Scheme (RB-IOS)

Launched in November 2021, the Reserve Bank Integrated Ombudsman Scheme provides a single grievance-redress window for customers of banks, non-banking financial companies, and payment-system operators. It brought the earlier separate ombudsman schemes under one framework, allowing a complaint about deficient service, a disputed transaction, or an unresolved grievance to be filed through one channel and resolved by an impartial ombudsman.

2.5.2 MANI App

The Mobile Aided Note Identifier (MANI) app, launched in January 2020, helps visually impaired users identify the denomination of banknotes by scanning them with a phone camera. It gives audio output in Hindi and English, works offline, and is free on both Android and iOS.

2.5.3 Retail Direct

The Retail Direct scheme, launched in November 2021, lets individual investors buy and hold government securities directly with the Reserve Bank, without going through a bank or broker. It widens access to a safe class of investment that was once open mainly to institutions.

2.5.4 UDGAM

The UDGAM portal (Unclaimed Deposits, Gateway to Access Information), launched in 2023, helps people search for unclaimed deposits across banks in one place and then approach the relevant bank to claim them.

2.5.5 PRAVAAH

The PRAVAAH portal (Platform for Regulatory Application, Validation, and Authorisation), launched in May 2024, lets individuals and firms apply online for the Reserve Bank's regulatory approvals, track their applications, and respond to queries through a single interface.

2.5.6 Awareness Initiatives: RBI Kehta Hai and the RBI Museum

Through the "RBI Kehta Hai" campaign the Reserve Bank educates the public on safe banking, digital transactions, and fraud prevention. The RBI Museum, in Kolkata, preserves the monetary history of the country and explains the evolution of currency and central banking to visitors.

2.6 Key Legislations Administered by the RBI

Several statutes give the Reserve Bank its powers and define the framework within which the financial system operates.

Reserve Bank of India Act, 1934: the founding law that establishes the Reserve Bank and grants its powers over monetary policy, currency, and the supervision of banks.

Banking Regulation Act, 1949: the principal law governing the licensing, management, and supervision of banks, including prudential norms, mergers, and resolution.

Payment and Settlement Systems Act, 2007: the law that empowers the Reserve Bank to authorise and regulate all payment systems in the country.

SARFAESI Act, 2002: which lets banks and financial institutions enforce security interests and recover dues from defaulters without a court order, aiding the recovery of non-performing assets.

Factoring Regulation Act, 2011: which regulates the factoring business, helping enterprises raise working capital by selling their receivables.

Credit Information Companies (Regulation) Act, 2005: which governs the credit-information companies that maintain borrowers' credit histories.

National Housing Bank Act, 1987: which created the National Housing Bank. Note that since 9 August 2019 the regulation of housing finance companies has rested with the Reserve Bank, not the National Housing Bank, with housing finance companies treated as a category of non-banking financial company; the National Housing Bank now supervises and refinances the sector.

2.7 Financial Inclusion

2.7.1 National Strategies

The Reserve Bank guides financial inclusion through two national strategies. The National Strategy for Financial Inclusion (2019-2024) aimed at universal access to financial services, greater affordability and availability, and effective use of those services. The complementary National Strategy for Financial Education (2020-2025) focuses on equipping people with the knowledge to budget, save, invest, insure, and plan for retirement.

2.7.2 Lead Bank Scheme and State Level Bankers' Committees

The Lead Bank Scheme, introduced in December 1969 on the recommendation of the Gadgil Study Group, assigns a lead bank to each district to coordinate banking development and prepare district credit plans. At the state level, State Level Bankers' Committees (SLBCs) bring together banks, the Reserve Bank, and government agencies to coordinate inclusion programmes, monitor schemes such as the Pradhan Mantri Jan Dhan Yojana, and report progress.

2.8 Payment and Settlement Infrastructure

Beyond retail payments, the Reserve Bank oversees the wholesale market utilities that clear and settle high-value and securities transactions.

RTGS (Real-Time Gross Settlement): introduced in 2004 for the immediate, irrevocable settlement of large-value payments on a one-to-one basis; it operates around the clock.

NEFT (National Electronic Funds Transfer): introduced in 2005 for one-to-one transfers settled in frequent batches; widely used for everyday remittances and now available at all hours.

NDS-OM and the CCIL: the Negotiated Dealing System-Order Matching platform (2005) for trading government securities, and the Clearing Corporation of India Ltd (2001), which clears and guarantees trades in government securities, money, and foreign-exchange markets as a central counterparty.

TReDS (Trade Receivables Discounting System): an electronic platform, operational since 2017, that lets micro, small, and medium enterprises raise working capital by discounting their unpaid invoices with financiers.

Electronic Trading Platforms and Trade Repositories: regulated venues for trading securities and derivatives, and centralised databases that record trades to support transparency and risk monitoring.

2.9 Financial Stability and Development Council (FSDC)

The Financial Stability and Development Council (FSDC) is the apex body for financial stability and inter-regulatory coordination, set up by the Government in 2010 following the Raghuram Rajan Committee on financial-sector reforms. Chaired by the Union Finance Minister, it monitors systemic risks, promotes inter-regulatory coordination, and oversees financial-sector development and inclusion. Its Sub-Committee, chaired by the Governor of the Reserve Bank, handles day-to-day coordination and brings together the financial-sector regulators, the Reserve Bank, SEBI, IRDAI, and PFRDA, along with the Insolvency and Bankruptcy Board of India.

2.10 International Financial Services Centres Authority (IFSCA)

The International Financial Services Centres Authority (IFSCA) was established on 27 April 2020 under the IFSCA Act, 2019, to develop and regulate International Financial Services Centres in the country, the foremost being GIFT City in Gujarat. It is a unified regulator that exercises, within these centres, the powers otherwise held by the Reserve Bank, SEBI, IRDAI, and PFRDA. It licenses entities, develops the financial-services ecosystem, supports fintech, and cooperates with foreign regulators.

2.11 National Payments Corporation of India (NPCI)

The National Payments Corporation of India (NPCI) is the umbrella organisation for retail payments. It was incorporated in 2008 as a not-for-profit company, promoted by the Reserve Bank of India and the Indian Banks' Association, under the Payment and Settlement Systems Act, 2007. NPCI builds and operates the infrastructure that has transformed how the country pays, from card payments and instant transfers to bill payments and toll collection.

2.11.1 Retail Payment Systems Operated by NPCI

National Financial Switch (NFS): the network that connects banks' ATMs, enabling cash withdrawal and balance enquiry across banks.

IMPS (Immediate Payment Service): launched in 2010, a round-the-clock service for instant interbank transfers through mobile, internet, and ATM channels.

RuPay: the domestic card network launched in 2012, providing a home-grown alternative to international card schemes for debit, credit, and prepaid cards.

NACH (National Automated Clearing House): a platform for bulk, recurring payments such as salaries, dividends, and bill collections; introduced by NPCI in 2012, it fully replaced the older electronic clearing service from 2016.

AEPS (Aadhaar Enabled Payment System): a biometric, Aadhaar-based system that allows basic banking transactions, valuable in rural areas with limited banking infrastructure.

CTS (Cheque Truncation System): electronic clearing of cheques using their images, which speeds settlement and reduces the risks of handling paper.

UPI (Unified Payments Interface): launched in 2016, a real-time system that links multiple bank accounts to a single mobile app and has become the country's dominant mode of digital payment.

NETC (National Electronic Toll Collection): the FASTag-based system that allows cashless, non-stop toll payment at highway plazas.

2.11.2 NPCI Subsidiaries

NPCI Bharat BillPay Ltd (NBBL): incorporated in 2020, it runs the Bharat Bill Payment System, an interoperable platform covering electricity, telecom, insurance, and other bills.

NPCI International Payments Ltd (NIPL): incorporated in 2020 to take UPI, RuPay, and other systems to overseas markets and to build cross-border payment links.

NPCI BHIM Services Ltd (NBSL): created in 2024 to manage and develop the BHIM app in a competitive UPI market.

2.12 RBI-Regulated Entities

The Reserve Bank regulates a wide range of institutions that take deposits, extend credit, and provide financial services. The most important of these are banks, which fall into several distinct types, along with non-banking financial companies and a small group of development institutions.

2.12.1 Classification of Banks

Banks are first divided into scheduled and non-scheduled banks. Scheduled banks are those listed in the Second Schedule of the Reserve Bank of India Act, 1934; they meet the conditions the Act lays down and are entitled to borrow from the Reserve Bank and to other facilities. Non-scheduled banks are not listed in that schedule and are few in number. Scheduled banks include both commercial banks and cooperative banks.

2.12.2 Commercial Banks

Commercial banks are the mainstay of the banking system, offering deposits, loans, and payment services. They are of three kinds:

Public sector banks: banks in which the Government of India holds a majority stake. Their number was reduced to twelve following the consolidation of public sector banks that took effect on 1 April 2020.

Private sector banks: banks owned mainly by private shareholders, which compete on service, technology, and reach.

Foreign banks: banks incorporated outside the country that operate in India through branches or wholly owned subsidiaries, under conditions set by the Reserve Bank.

2.12.3 Regional Rural Banks and Local Area Banks

Regional Rural Banks (RRBs): banks established under the Regional Rural Banks Act, 1976, to meet the credit needs of agriculture and the rural economy. Each RRB is sponsored by a commercial bank and is jointly owned by the Central Government, the sponsor bank, and the State Government; it is regulated by the Reserve Bank and supervised and refinanced by NABARD.

Local Area Banks: small private banks licensed to operate within a few neighbouring districts, intended to mobilise local savings and lend within the same area.

2.12.4 Small Finance Banks

Small finance banks were introduced under Reserve Bank guidelines issued in 2014, with the first such banks beginning operations in 2016, and on-tap licensing opened in 2019. Their purpose is to serve small and under-served customers, small businesses, marginal and small farmers, and the unorganised sector. They accept deposits and lend like other banks, but must meet special obligations: a large share of their lending must go to the priority sector (sixty per cent of adjusted net bank credit, as on the financial year 2025-26), and a major part of their loan book must consist of small-value loans. Examples include AU, Ujjivan, and Equitas small finance banks.

2.12.5 Payments Banks

Payments banks were introduced under Reserve Bank guidelines issued in 2014, on the recommendation of the Nachiket Mor Committee, with the first such banks beginning operations from 2016. They are designed to widen access to basic banking and digital payments, especially for low-income households, migrant workers, and small businesses. A payments bank can accept deposits (up to a limit per customer set by the Reserve Bank, two lakh rupees as on April 2021), offer payments and remittance services, and issue debit cards, but it cannot lend or issue credit cards. Examples include Airtel Payments Bank, India Post Payments Bank, and Fino Payments Bank.

2.12.6 Cooperative Banks

Cooperative banks serve local and rural communities on cooperative principles. They comprise urban cooperative banks and a three-tier rural credit structure: Primary Agricultural Credit Societies at the village level, District Central Cooperative Banks at the district level, and State Cooperative Banks at the apex of each state. The precise position on who oversees them matters. Following the Banking Regulation (Amendment) Act, 2020, the Reserve Bank is the banking regulator of state and district central cooperative banks, while NABARD supervises and refinances them. The primary societies fall under state cooperative law and outside the Reserve Bank's banking regulation. In short, the Reserve Bank regulates and NABARD supervises, and the two roles should not be confused.

2.12.7 Non-Banking Financial Companies (NBFCs)

Non-banking financial companies provide credit and other financial services such as leasing, hire-purchase, investment, and microfinance, but they cannot accept demand deposits or take part in the payment system as banks do. They range from loan companies and infrastructure finance companies to microfinance institutions and housing finance companies. The Reserve Bank regulates them under a scale-based framework, which applies progressively stricter rules to larger and more systemically important companies.

2.12.8 All-India Financial Institutions (AIFIs)

A small group of development institutions is regulated directly by the Reserve Bank as all-India financial institutions: the Export-Import Bank of India, NABARD, the National Housing Bank, SIDBI, and NABFID. These supply long-term and directed finance to areas such as exports, agriculture, housing, small industry, and infrastructure, and are profiled in Chapter 3.

Profiles of Public Financial Institutions

India's development needs are served not only by its regulators and commercial banks but also by a set of specialised, mostly Government-owned institutions that supply long-term and directed finance to areas the ordinary market serves poorly: infrastructure, exports, small industry, housing, and agriculture. These are the public financial institutions profiled in this chapter. Each was created by statute or by the Government to pursue a defined developmental purpose, and several are supervised by the Reserve Bank of India as all-India financial institutions. The profiles below set out, for each body, when and how it was established, who owns and regulates it, what it does, and where it stands today.

3.1 India Infrastructure Finance Company Ltd. (IIFCL)

India Infrastructure Finance Company Ltd. (IIFCL) is a wholly Government-owned company that provides long-term finance for infrastructure projects which commercial lenders find difficult to fund. It was incorporated on 5 January 2006 under the Companies Act, 1956, and works under the Ministry of Finance. Since September 2013 it has been registered with the Reserve Bank of India as a non-deposit-taking infrastructure finance company (NBFC-IFC). Its registered office is in New Delhi.

3.1.1 Establishment and Mandate

IIFCL was created to bridge the country's infrastructure financing gap, where the long gestation periods and high risks of large projects deterred conventional lenders. Operating mainly under the Scheme for Financing Viable Infrastructure Projects (SIFTI), it provides long-term debt to viable projects in transport, energy, water, urban infrastructure, and telecommunications, giving priority to public-private partnership (PPP) projects. It also supports national programmes such as the National Infrastructure Pipeline and the PM Gati Shakti National Master Plan. Its authorised capital stood at ₹10,000 crore and paid-up capital at about ₹9,999.92 crore as on 31 March 2025.

3.1.2 Functions and Financial Products

IIFCL's assistance takes several forms:

Direct lending: long-term loans, typically of ten to twenty-five years, for greenfield and brownfield infrastructure projects.

Takeout finance and refinance: taking over project loans from banks once a project is operational, and refinancing lenders, which frees their capital for fresh lending.

Subordinate debt: mezzanine funding that strengthens a project's capital structure and helps it raise senior debt.

Credit enhancement: partial guarantees that raise the credit rating of infrastructure bonds, helping projects tap insurers and pension funds.

Green and sustainable finance: funding for renewable energy and other environmentally beneficial projects, including through green bonds.

3.1.3 Subsidiaries

IIFC (UK) Limited: incorporated in London on 7 February 2008 with an authorised capital of USD 500 million, it lends to Indian companies for the import of capital goods for infrastructure projects in India and is registered with the United Kingdom regulator as an Annex-I financial institution.

IIFCL Asset Management Company Limited (IAMCL): manages the IIFCL Mutual Fund, an Infrastructure Debt Fund that channels long-term institutional investment into infrastructure.

IIFCL Projects Limited (IPL): provides advisory and project-development services.

3.1.4 Recent Developments

IIFCL reported record results in 2024-25, with profit after tax of about ₹2,165 crore and sanctions exceeding ₹51,000 crore. The Government has approved an initial public offering, with a stock-market listing expected in the coming years.

3.2 Export-Import Bank of India (EXIM Bank)

The Export-Import Bank of India (EXIM Bank) is the country's principal export credit agency. It was established under the Export-Import Bank of India Act, 1981, and commenced operations in March 1982. It is wholly owned by the Government of India, regulated by the Reserve Bank of India as an all-India financial institution, and headquartered in Mumbai.

3.2.1 Establishment and Mandate

EXIM Bank was set up to finance, facilitate, and promote India's foreign trade and to support the international expansion of Indian businesses. Its mandate covers:

Export finance: providing credit to exporters and to overseas buyers of Indian goods and services.

Lines of credit: extending Government-backed lines of credit to foreign governments and institutions, which they use to purchase Indian goods and services.

Project exports: financing Indian firms that execute turnkey projects, construction contracts, and consultancy assignments abroad.

Trade facilitation and advisory: research, market information, and guidance that help Indian enterprises enter new markets.

3.2.2 Financial Products and Services

To carry out this mandate the bank offers a range of products:

Buyer's and supplier's credit: financing that allows overseas buyers to pay for Indian exports over time.

Term loans for export-oriented units: funding for capacity creation and modernisation in export industries.

Overseas investment finance: loans and equity support for Indian companies setting up ventures or acquiring assets abroad.

Ubharte Sitaare Programme: support for export-oriented micro, small, and medium enterprises with strong potential.

Guarantees and advisory services: instruments and counsel that help exporters manage payment, currency, and country risks.

3.2.3 Recent Developments

Parliament raised the bank's authorised capital to ₹20,000 crore in 2019. EXIM Bank operates supporting entities, including an asset-management company and a unit at GIFT City, and has been expanding its overseas presence to deepen India's trade ties, particularly with Africa.

3.3 Small Industries Development Bank of India (SIDBI)

The Small Industries Development Bank of India (SIDBI) is the country's principal financial institution for the promotion, financing, and development of the micro, small, and medium enterprise (MSME) sector. It was established on 2 April 1990 under the Small Industries Development Bank of India Act, 1989, and is headquartered in Lucknow. Although set up as a wholly owned subsidiary of the Industrial Development Bank of India (IDBI), it was delinked in 2000 and is now jointly owned by the Government of India together with the State Bank of India, the Life Insurance Corporation of India, and several other banks and institutions. It is supervised by the Reserve Bank of India as an all-India financial institution.

3.3.1 Establishment and Mandate

SIDBI was created to give India's vast small-enterprise sector a dedicated source of finance and developmental support. Its work rests on three pillars: refinancing the institutions that lend to MSMEs, lending directly to MSMEs, and strengthening the wider ecosystem in which small businesses operate.

3.3.2 Functions and Financial Products

Indirect (refinance) lending: to banks, non-banking financial companies, and microfinance institutions that on-lend to MSMEs.

Direct lending: to MSMEs for term loans, working capital, and specific needs such as energy efficiency and technology upgrading.

Fund-of-funds: investing in venture funds that back start-ups, including as the operating agency for the Government's Fund of Funds for Start-ups.

Promotion and development: skill-building, cluster development, and digital platforms such as Udyamimitra that connect entrepreneurs with lenders.

3.3.3 Subsidiaries and Associates

MUDRA: the Micro Units Development and Refinance Agency, which refinances lending to the smallest borrowers.

SIDBI Venture Capital Limited: which manages venture and growth-capital funds for smaller enterprises.

Acuité Ratings & Research: a credit-rating associate (formerly SMERA).

SIDBI also operates the Credit Guarantee Fund Trust for Micro and Small Enterprises (CGTMSE) jointly with the Ministry of Micro, Small and Medium Enterprises, which provides collateral-free credit guarantees to small borrowers.

3.4 National Housing Bank (NHB)

The National Housing Bank (NHB) is the apex institution for housing finance in India. It was set up on 9 July 1988 under the National Housing Bank Act, 1987. NHB was originally wholly owned by the Reserve Bank of India; in 2019 the Reserve Bank transferred its entire shareholding to the Government of India, so the bank is now fully Government-owned. Its head office is in New Delhi.

3.4.1 Establishment and Changed Role

NHB was established to promote housing finance institutions and to direct resources into the housing sector. Its role changed significantly in 2019. Until then, NHB was the regulator of housing finance companies (HFCs); with effect from 9 August 2019, that regulatory responsibility passed to the Reserve Bank of India, which now registers and regulates HFCs as a category of non-banking financial company. NHB today performs two principal functions: it supervises HFCs through on-site inspection and off-site surveillance, and it acts as the apex provider of refinance for housing loans. In short, the Reserve Bank now regulates HFCs, while NHB supervises them and finances the sector.

3.4.2 Functions

Refinance: providing long-term funds to banks and housing finance companies against their housing loans.

Supervision: inspecting and monitoring housing finance companies, within the regulatory framework now set by the Reserve Bank.

Resource mobilisation and securitisation: raising funds through bonds and pioneering mortgage-backed securitisation in India.

Government schemes and information: implementing housing-subsidy schemes such as the credit-linked subsidy under the Pradhan Mantri Awas Yojana, and publishing the NHB RESIDEX house-price index.

3.4.3 Recent Developments

Following the 2019 changes, the Reserve Bank issued a revised regulatory framework for housing finance companies in 2020. NHB continues to supervise the sector and to channel refinance into affordable housing.

3.5 National Bank for Agriculture and Rural Development (NABARD)

The National Bank for Agriculture and Rural Development (NABARD) is the apex development bank for agriculture and the rural economy. It came into existence on 12 July 1982 under the National Bank for Agriculture and Rural Development Act, 1981, taking over the agricultural-credit functions of the Reserve

Bank of India and the refinance functions of the former Agricultural Refinance and Development Corporation. The Reserve Bank's residual shareholding was transferred to the Government of India in 2019, so NABARD is now wholly Government-owned. Its head office is in Mumbai.

3.5.1 Establishment and Mandate

NABARD was set up to provide and regulate credit for agriculture, small-scale industry, cottage and village industries, handicrafts, and other rural crafts, and more broadly to promote integrated rural development. It pursues this through refinance, direct financing of rural infrastructure, supervision of the rural banking system, and a wide range of developmental programmes.

3.5.2 Functions

Refinance: extending refinance to cooperative banks, regional rural banks, and other institutions that lend for farm and rural activity.

Rural Infrastructure Development Fund (RIDF): financing rural roads, irrigation, and other infrastructure through state governments.

Supervision: conducting statutory inspection of cooperative banks and regional rural banks.

Developmental work: running the Self-Help Group-Bank Linkage Programme, watershed and tribal-development projects, and support for farmer producer organisations.

3.5.3 Subsidiaries

NABARD operates through several subsidiaries that extend its developmental reach, including NABKISAN Finance, NABSAMRUDDHI Finance, NABFINS, NABCONS (its consultancy arm), NABVENTURES, NABFOUNDATION, and NABSanrakshan.

3.6 Industrial Finance Corporation of India (IFCI)

The Industrial Finance Corporation of India (IFCI) was India's first development financial institution. It was established on 1 July 1948 under the Industrial Finance Corporation Act, 1948, to provide medium- and long-term finance to industry. In 1993 it was converted from a statutory corporation into a company, IFCI Limited, under the Companies Act. The Government of India is now the majority shareholder, IFCI having become a Government company in 2015. It is registered with the Reserve Bank as a systemically important non-deposit-taking non-banking financial company and is headquartered in New Delhi.

3.6.1 From Statutory Corporation to Government Company

For its first four decades IFCI was the principal channel of long-term industrial finance in the country, supporting the creation of capacity across core industries. After the financial-sector reforms of the early 1990s it was converted into a company so that it could raise capital from the market and compete with other lenders. Government shareholding rose over time, and in 2015 IFCI became a Government company; the Government has since made further capital infusions.

3.6.2 Current Position

Having historically provided project and corporate loans, IFCI stopped fresh lending from 2021-22 and is transitioning into an advisory and nodal-agency role. It serves as the nodal agency for Government schemes such as Production-Linked Incentive programmes and the Sugar Development Fund. The Government has also approved a consolidation of the IFCI group, bringing together IFCI Limited and associated entities, including the Stock Holding Corporation of India.

3.7 National Bank for Financing Infrastructure and Development (NABFID)

The National Bank for Financing Infrastructure and Development (NABFID) is India's newest development financial institution. It was established in 2021 under the National Bank for Financing Infrastructure and Development Act, 2021. It is owned by the Government of India, regulated by the Reserve Bank of India as an all-India financial institution, and headquartered in Mumbai. NABFID is the fifth such institution, alongside EXIM Bank, NABARD, NHB, and SIDBI, and marks the return of dedicated development banking for infrastructure after a gap of many years.

3.7.1 Establishment and Mandate

NABFID was set up to provide long-term, non-recourse finance for infrastructure and to help develop the bonds and derivatives markets that such financing requires. It has an authorised share capital of ₹1 lakh crore, and the Government provided initial paid-up capital of ₹20,000 crore together with a grant of ₹5,000 crore. Its founding Chairperson is K. V. Kamath and its Managing Director is Rajkiran Rai G.

3.7.2 Functions

Long-term project loans: non-recourse finance for infrastructure projects across sectors.

Credit enhancement and takeout finance: support that improves the bankability of projects and refinances existing lenders.

Equity and quasi-equity: investment that strengthens the capital base of infrastructure ventures.

Market development: building the infrastructure bond and derivatives markets to draw long-term private capital.

3.7.3 Recent Developments

NABFID commenced operations in December 2022, and its cumulative sanctions crossed the ₹1 trillion mark by March 2024, within about fifteen months of starting business, a rapid scaling-up that reflects the scale of India's infrastructure financing needs.

CHAPTER 4

Entities under SEBI: Financial Markets

The securities markets bring together those who need capital and those who have it to invest, and a wide range of institutions and intermediaries make that meeting safe and orderly. At the apex sits the Securities and Exchange Board of India (SEBI), which regulates the whole structure: the exchanges where securities trade, the depositories that hold them, the clearing corporations that settle trades, the intermediaries who serve investors, the pooled vehicles through which people invest, and the bodies that support the industry. This chapter profiles each in turn.

4.1 Securities and Exchange Board of India (SEBI)

The Securities and Exchange Board of India (SEBI) is the regulator of the securities and commodity-derivatives markets. Its purpose is to protect investors, to develop the market, and to regulate those who operate in it so that trading is fair, transparent, and efficient. Its head office is in Mumbai.

4.1.1 Establishment and Statutory Basis

In the 1980s the securities markets were lightly regulated and dogged by insider trading, price manipulation, and poor disclosure. SEBI was set up in 1988 as a non-statutory body to address these problems, and on 30 January 1992 it was given full statutory powers under the SEBI Act, 1992, which marks the beginning of formal regulation of the market.

4.1.2 Objectives and Functions

SEBI pursues three broad aims, protecting investors, regulating the market, and developing it:

Investor protection: guarding investors against fraud, insider trading, and manipulation, and requiring honest disclosure so they can make informed decisions.

Regulation of the market and its participants: overseeing exchanges, depositories, clearing corporations, brokers, mutual funds, and other intermediaries, and ensuring they meet professional and ethical standards.

Market development: introducing reforms and products that improve efficiency and draw in domestic and foreign investors.

Regulation of public offerings: governing initial and follow-on public offerings and rights issues, with full disclosure of relevant information.

Enforcement: investigating wrongdoing and imposing penalties, suspensions, or prosecution where the law is broken.

4.1.3 Principal Laws and Regulations

SEBI draws its authority from, and enforces, a body of securities law. The chief statutes are the SEBI Act, 1992 (its charter and powers), the Securities Contracts (Regulation) Act, 1956 (recognition and regulation of stock exchanges), and the Depositories Act, 1996 (dematerialisation of securities). Working under these, SEBI frames regulations covering insider trading, substantial acquisitions and takeovers, mutual funds, listing obligations and disclosure, and many categories of intermediary; it also works with the Companies Act, 2013 on corporate governance and disclosure for listed companies.

4.1.4 Major Contributions

Electronic trading: SEBI promoted screen-based trading, replacing the open-outcry floor and making the market faster and more transparent.

Corporate governance: the governance norms once contained in Clause 49 of the listing agreement, and now in the listing-disclosure regulations, raised the accountability of listed companies.

A modern mutual-fund framework: the mutual-fund regulations gave the industry a clear and protective structure within which it grew rapidly.

Investor protection and education: SEBI maintains its own Investor Protection and Education Fund and runs awareness programmes. (The separate Investor Education and Protection Fund is administered by the Ministry of Corporate Affairs, not SEBI.)

Sustainable finance: SEBI has introduced disclosure norms for environmental, social, and governance (ESG) factors to support responsible investing.

4.1.5 Leadership and Structure

SEBI is headed by a Chairman appointed by the Government of India, with a board that includes nominees of the Ministry of Finance and the Reserve Bank along with other members. Its departments handle policy, surveillance, enforcement, and investor education.

4.1.6 Market Segments SEBI Oversees

Equity Segment

The market in company shares, where ownership is bought and sold and prices are set by supply and demand; participants range from retail investors to mutual funds and foreign investors.

Derivatives Segment

The market in futures and options, whose value derives from an underlying share, index, or commodity; these contracts are used to hedge risk and to speculate, and they allow leverage, control of a large position with a smaller outlay, which magnifies both gains and losses.

Commodity Segment

The market in commodity derivatives, bullion, energy, metals, and agricultural produce, used by producers and consumers to hedge price risk and by traders for price discovery. SEBI has regulated this segment since the Forward Markets Commission merged into it in 2015.

4.2 Recognised Stock Exchanges

Stock exchanges provide the regulated venues where securities and derivatives are listed and traded, offering price discovery, liquidity, and a transparent order-matching mechanism. The principal recognised exchanges are profiled below.

4.2.1 BSE Ltd (Bombay Stock Exchange)

Established in 1875, the BSE is the oldest stock exchange in Asia. Headquartered in Mumbai, it lists thousands of companies and trades equities, derivatives, and debt. Its benchmark index, the Sensex, tracks 30 leading companies and is a widely followed barometer of the market. The BSE was the first Indian exchange to dematerialise shares and to launch a dedicated platform for small and medium enterprises.

4.2.2 National Stock Exchange of India Ltd (NSE)

Incorporated in 1992 and operational from 1994, the NSE is the largest exchange in the country by trading volume. Based in Mumbai, it pioneered fully electronic, screen-based trading. Its Nifty 50 index is the leading equity benchmark, and it dominates equity-derivatives trading; it also offers currency and interest-rate derivatives.

4.2.3 Other Exchanges

Calcutta Stock Exchange (CSE): established in 1908 in Kolkata, one of the oldest exchanges, though its trading activity has declined sharply with the rise of the national exchanges.

Metropolitan Stock Exchange of India (MSEI): established in 2008 (formerly the MCX Stock Exchange), a smaller national exchange offering equity, derivative, and currency products.

4.2.4 Commodity Derivatives Exchanges

Multi Commodity Exchange of India (MCX): established in 2003, the largest commodity-derivatives exchange, strongest in bullion and energy.

National Commodity & Derivatives Exchange (NCDEX): established in 2003, the leading exchange for agricultural commodity derivatives, where it helps farmers and traders hedge price risk.

4.3 Depositories

Depositories hold securities in electronic form and enable their transfer without paper certificates, which makes trading faster and safer. Investors hold their securities in demat accounts opened through depository participants. The country has two depositories.

4.3.1 National Securities Depository Limited (NSDL)

Established in 1996, NSDL was the first depository in the country and the institution that introduced dematerialisation. It was promoted by the Industrial Development Bank of India, the BSE, and the NSE. It holds and transfers securities electronically, settles trades, and processes corporate actions such as dividends and bonus issues. NSDL was itself listed on the stock exchange in 2025.

4.3.2 Central Depository Services Limited (CDSL)

Established in 1999 and promoted by the BSE, CDSL provides the same depository services to retail and institutional investors. It became the first listed depository when it went public in 2017, and it holds the larger number of demat accounts in the country.

4.4 Recognised Clearing Corporations

A clearing corporation settles the trades executed on an exchange and removes the risk that one side fails to deliver. It does this by acting as the central counterparty, becoming the buyer to every seller and the seller to every buyer, so that a trade settles even if one party defaults. To support this guarantee it collects margins, manages collateral, and maintains a settlement guarantee fund. Because these functions are common to all of them, the recognised clearing corporations are listed here with their year of formation and their parent exchange:

NSE Clearing Ltd (NCL): formed in 1995 (formerly the National Securities Clearing Corporation), the clearing arm of the NSE, covering equities, derivatives, and debt.

Indian Clearing Corporation Ltd (ICCL): formed in 2007, a subsidiary of the BSE that clears trades executed on it.

National Commodity Clearing Ltd (NCCL): formed in 2006, the clearing corporation for the NCDEX commodity market.

Multi Commodity Exchange Clearing Corporation (MCX-CC): formed in 2018, the clearing arm of the MCX.

AMC Repo Clearing Ltd (AMCRCL): formed in 2021, a specialised corporation that clears and settles repo transactions in corporate debt.

4.5 Market Intermediaries

Intermediaries connect investors to the markets and provide the advice and analysis that inform investment decisions. All of them are registered with and regulated by SEBI, which sets standards of conduct, disclosure, and capital.

4.5.1 Stock Brokers and Sub-Brokers

Brokers execute buy and sell orders on the exchanges on behalf of clients, across the equity, derivatives, and commodity segments, and handle the settlement of those trades. Many also offer research and advice. Some provide margin facilities, allowing clients to take leveraged positions, larger than their own capital would permit, which raises both potential return and risk. Brokers fall into two broad types: full-service brokers, who add research, advisory, and portfolio services; and discount brokers, who focus on low-cost order execution. Sub-brokers act under a broker to serve retail investors.

4.5.2 Portfolio Managers

Portfolio managers build and run investment portfolios for individuals and institutions according to each client's goals and risk appetite. They decide asset allocation, select securities, manage risk, and report on performance, and they work mainly for high-net-worth and institutional clients.

4.5.3 Investment Advisers

Investment advisers give tailored advice on investments and financial planning after assessing a client's goals, risk tolerance, and circumstances. Registered with SEBI, they are expected to act transparently; the fee-based model, in which the adviser is paid by the client rather than by product commissions, is regarded as the more conflict-free.

4.5.4 Research Analysts

Research analysts study companies, industries, and the wider economy and publish recommendations on which investment decisions are based. Whether using fundamental analysis of a company's financials or technical analysis of price and volume, they are required by SEBI to produce unbiased and transparent research.

4.6 Issuer-Side and Debt-Market Intermediaries

A further set of intermediaries supports the issue of securities and the working of the debt market.

Merchant bankers: help companies raise capital through public offerings and private placements and advise on mergers and restructuring.

Registrars to an issue and share-transfer agents: manage the application and allotment process and maintain accurate records of shareholders.

Bankers to an issue: collect application money for securities issues and handle allotment and refund flows.

Debenture trustees: protect debenture-holders by ensuring the issuer meets its obligations to pay interest and principal.

Credit rating agencies: assess the creditworthiness of issuers and debt instruments, guiding investors on the risk of a bond.

Custodians: safekeep securities for institutional investors, settle their trades, and manage corporate actions on their behalf.

Online bond platform providers: digital platforms that give retail investors direct, transparent access to the bond market.

4.7 Pooled Investment Vehicles

Pooled vehicles gather money from many investors and invest it collectively, giving access to diversification and professional management. All are regulated by SEBI.

4.7.1 Mutual Funds

Mutual funds pool money from investors and invest it, according to a stated objective, in a diversified portfolio of shares, bonds, and money-market instruments managed by professional fund managers. They come in several types, equity, debt, hybrid, index, and liquid funds, and offer features such as Systematic Investment Plans (SIPs), which let investors put in a fixed sum regularly. They are governed by the SEBI (Mutual Funds) Regulations, 1996, under which each fund operates through an independent trustee and an asset-management company, must register its schemes, disclose its strategy and risks in an offer document, publish its net asset value daily, and follow SEBI's norms on valuation, risk management, and advertising.

4.7.2 Alternative Investment Funds (AIFs)

AIFs pool capital, usually from high-net-worth and institutional investors, to invest in less liquid assets such as private equity, venture capital, hedge-fund strategies, and distressed assets, in pursuit of higher returns at higher risk.

4.7.3 REITs and InvITs

Real Estate Investment Trusts (REITs) and Infrastructure Investment Trusts (InvITs) pool money to invest in income-generating real estate and infrastructure respectively. Listed on the exchanges, they pass most of their rental or operating income to investors and give access, with liquidity, to assets that are otherwise hard for individuals to hold.

4.7.4 Venture Capital Investors

Venture Capital Funds provide equity finance to start-ups and early-stage companies with high growth potential, often adding mentorship and networks. Foreign Venture Capital Investors are overseas entities that bring foreign capital and expertise into Indian start-ups on the same lines.

4.8 Other Specialised Entities

Self-Certified Syndicate Banks (ASBA): banks that let investors apply for public issues with the application money blocked in their own accounts until allotment, under the Application Supported by Blocked Amount facility.

Designated and Qualified Depository Participants: participants that open demat accounts and handle the dematerialisation and settlement of securities, including for foreign investors.

Vault managers: entities that store and manage the physical gold backing instruments such as electronic gold receipts.

ESG rating providers: agencies that rate companies on environmental, social, and governance performance to guide responsible investors.

4.9 Industry and Predecessor Bodies

4.9.1 Association of Mutual Funds in India (AMFI)

AMFI is the industry body of the mutual-fund sector, established in 1995 with the support of SEBI and the fund houses. A not-for-profit association, it promotes mutual funds, sets a code of conduct, standardises industry practice, represents the industry to regulators, and has driven the spread of investor education and of Systematic Investment Plans.

4.9.2 Forward Markets Commission (FMC) and its Merger with SEBI

The Forward Markets Commission was the regulator of commodity-futures markets, established in 1953 under the Forward Contracts (Regulation) Act, 1952. In 2015 it was merged into SEBI, bringing commodity-derivatives regulation under the same authority that oversees the securities market and giving the country a single regulator for both. SEBI now regulates the commodity-derivatives exchanges that the Commission once supervised.

CHAPTER 5

Entities under IRDAI: Insurance

Insurance lets individuals and businesses transfer risk, of death, illness, accident, or loss of property, to a pooled fund in return for a premium. The sector is overseen by a single regulator, the Insurance Regulatory and Development Authority of India (IRDAI), and is made up of life insurers, general and health insurers, reinsurers, a wide range of intermediaries who connect insurers to customers, and the professional and industry bodies that support them. This chapter profiles the regulator and the principal entities under it.

5.1 Insurance Regulatory and Development Authority of India (IRDAI)

IRDAI is the apex body that regulates and develops the insurance sector. It was constituted under the Insurance Regulatory and Development Authority Act, 1999, and became operational as an autonomous Authority in 2000, building on the foundational Insurance Act, 1938. It works under the Ministry of Finance and is headquartered in Hyderabad. Its twin aims, reflected in its name, are to regulate insurers prudently and to develop the market so that insurance reaches more of the population, all while protecting policyholders.

5.1.1 Regulation and Supervision of Insurers

IRDAI licenses every insurer and reinsurer and sets the prudential rules within which they must operate. It fixes capital requirements and solvency margins so that insurers can always meet their claims, lays down investment norms that direct a share of premiums into safe instruments such as government securities, and reviews products and their pricing so that cover is fair, clearly worded, and adequately priced for the risk. It monitors insurers' conduct in collecting premiums, issuing policies, and settling claims, and can act against those that fall short.

5.1.2 Protection of Policyholders

Safeguarding the policyholder is at the centre of IRDAI's work. It requires insurers to disclose terms honestly and to deal fairly, regulates the conduct of agents, brokers, and other intermediaries to prevent mis-selling, and maintains grievance-redress machinery, including the independent Insurance Ombudsman, so that disputes a customer cannot settle directly with an insurer can be taken further.

5.1.3 Development of the Sector

To widen the reach of insurance, IRDAI promotes financial literacy, encourages microinsurance and other affordable products designed for low-income and rural households, and supports digital distribution and claims. It also develops the domestic reinsurance market and frames the rules under which insurers innovate, so that the industry grows without compromising the security of policyholders.

5.1.4 Recent Developments

IRDAI has set the goal of "Insurance for All by 2047" and is pursuing it through the Bima Trinity, Bima Sugam, a digital insurance marketplace; Bima Vistaar, a simple bundled cover; and Bima Vahak, a rural, women-led distribution force, together with a faster "Use and File" route for clearing products. In December 2025 the law was amended to permit up to 100 per cent foreign direct investment in insurance companies, raised from the earlier limit of 74 per cent; the higher limit is subject to conditions to be prescribed by the Government, and its commencement is to be notified.

5.2 Life Insurers

Life insurers protect against the financial consequences of death and also offer savings, pension, and unit-linked products. The market has many private life insurers, but it is dominated by the public-sector Life Insurance Corporation.

5.2.1 Life Insurance Corporation of India (LIC)

LIC is the largest and oldest life insurer in the country. It was established in 1956 under the Life Insurance Corporation Act, 1956, when life insurance was nationalised, and it is headquartered in Mumbai. It offers the full range of life products, term cover, endowment and money-back plans, pensions, unit-linked plans, and child plans, and reaches deep into rural India through a vast agency network, which has made it a pillar of the country's social security. Once wholly Government-owned, LIC was listed on the stock exchanges after its initial public offering in 2022; the Government of India remains the majority owner, holding about 96.5 per cent of the equity as on early 2025. Like every insurer, it is regulated by IRDAI.

5.3 General (Non-Life) Insurers

General, or non-life, insurers cover risks other than death, motor, property, marine, fire, liability, travel, and crop. The segment includes private insurers, four public-sector general insurers (New India Assurance, Oriental Insurance, United India Insurance, and National Insurance), and specialised insurers, two of which are profiled below.

5.3.1 Agriculture Insurance Company of India (AIC)

AIC is a specialised, Government-owned insurer set up in 2002 to provide crop and other agricultural cover. It protects farmers against losses from drought, flood, hailstorm, cyclone, and pests, and is the principal implementing agency for national crop-insurance schemes, most recently the Pradhan Mantri Fasal Bima Yojana. Working with the Ministry of Agriculture and state governments, it has become central to managing agricultural risk, and like other insurers it is regulated by IRDAI.

5.3.2 ECGC Limited

ECGC (formerly the Export Credit Guarantee Corporation of India) was established in 1957 and is wholly owned by the Government of India. It provides export-credit insurance, protecting Indian exporters against the risk of non-payment by foreign buyers and against political and commercial risks abroad, and it backs the lending that banks extend to exporters. By covering these risks it gives Indian businesses the confidence to enter new overseas markets. As an insurer it is registered with and regulated by IRDAI.

5.4 Health Insurers

Health insurers meet the cost of hospitalisation, treatment, and related medical care, a fast-growing segment as healthcare costs rise. Cover is offered both by standalone health insurers and by general insurers, and ranges from individual and family-floater policies to critical-illness and cashless hospitalisation plans, typically including pre- and post-hospitalisation expenses and day-care procedures. Public health insurers, private insurers, and standalone health specialists all compete in this market, while Government schemes such as Ayushman Bharat extend health cover to economically weaker households. IRDAI regulates the segment to keep products transparent, portable between insurers, and fair to policyholders.

5.5 Reinsurers

Reinsurance is insurance for insurers: a primary insurer passes on part of its risk to a reinsurer, which lets it underwrite larger or more concentrated risks without threatening its own solvency. Reinsurance is what allows the market to absorb catastrophic losses from earthquakes, floods, or pandemics.

5.5.1 General Insurance Corporation of India (GIC Re)

GIC Re is the national reinsurer and the largest reinsurance company in the country. It was established in 1972 and is headquartered in Mumbai, and it is publicly owned. It accepts reinsurance across property, liability, marine, aviation, health, and crop lines from Indian and overseas insurers, and operates internationally across Asia, Africa, Europe, and the Middle East. By carrying a share of domestic insurers' risk it strengthens the stability and the risk-carrying capacity of the whole market. From 2025 the domestic reinsurance market began opening to private reinsurers as well.

5.5.2 Foreign Reinsurance Branches

Foreign Reinsurance Branches are the India branches of global reinsurers, licensed by IRDAI to write reinsurance within the country. They bring additional capacity, global expertise, and capital, helping Indian insurers place large and unusual risks. Major reinsurers operating through such branches include Swiss Re, Munich Re, and Lloyd's of London.

5.6 Insurance Intermediaries

Intermediaries connect insurers to customers and help policies to be sold, serviced, and claimed. All of them are registered with and regulated by IRDAI, which sets standards of conduct, training, and disclosure; the main types are profiled below.

5.6.1 Insurance Brokers

Brokers represent the customer rather than any single insurer. Drawing on access to many insurers and reinsurers, a broker assesses a client's needs, recommends suitable cover, negotiates terms, and assists at the time of a claim. Brokers may be retail (serving individuals), corporate (serving businesses with liability, property, and employee-benefit cover), or reinsurance brokers who arrange cover for insurers themselves.

5.6.2 Corporate Agents

Corporate agents are organisations, often banks or other companies, licensed to solicit and service insurance on behalf of insurers. Unlike a broker, a corporate agent works for the insurers it represents, and it may tie up with up to a limited number of life, general, and health insurers, distributing their products to its own customer base and handling issuance and renewals.

5.6.3 Surveyors and Loss Assessors

Surveyors and loss assessors are independent professionals who assess the cause and extent of a loss in general insurance claims, motor, fire, property, marine, and report an unbiased valuation to the insurer. Their objective assessment protects both insurer and policyholder and keeps claim settlement fair.

5.6.4 Web Aggregators

Web aggregators run digital platforms that let customers compare the premiums, cover, and terms of products from different insurers in one place and buy online. By presenting choices transparently they simplify the purchase decision; familiar examples include PolicyBazaar, Coverfox, and BankBazaar.

5.6.5 Third-Party Administrators (TPAs)

TPAs are intermediaries in health insurance that manage claims on behalf of insurers. They run the cashless hospitalisation process at network hospitals, settle claims with those hospitals directly, maintain the hospital network, and provide customer support, so that a policyholder can be treated without paying upfront.

5.6.6 Insurance Marketing Firms (IMFs)

IMFs are licensed firms that distribute the products of several insurers within a defined area, and may also offer related financial products. They widen distribution, particularly into smaller towns and under-served areas, but do not underwrite or settle claims themselves.

5.7 Grievance Redress: Bima Bharosa

Bima Bharosa is IRDAI's online grievance-redress system for policyholders. A customer who is unhappy about a rejected claim, a delay, or poor service can register a complaint through the portal, helpline, or email; the complaint is routed to the insurer concerned for resolution and tracked, and if it remains unresolved it can be escalated within IRDAI or taken to the Insurance Ombudsman. The system also helps educate consumers about their rights, and is a central part of consumer protection in the sector.

5.8 Professional and Industry Bodies

Several professional and industry bodies set standards, train practitioners, and represent the trade within the insurance sector.

5.8.1 Institute of Actuaries of India (IAI)

The IAI is the statutory body for the actuarial profession. It began in 1944 as the Actuarial Society of India and was incorporated under the Actuaries Act, 2006. It sets the education and examination path for actuaries, awards the Associate and Fellow qualifications, enforces a professional code of conduct, and represents actuaries across insurance, pensions, and finance, a profession central to pricing and reserving in insurance.

5.8.2 Insurance Brokers Association of India (IBAI)

IBAI, established on 25 July 2001, is the representative body of licensed insurance brokers. It speaks for brokers before IRDAI and other authorities, sets professional and ethical standards for its members, runs training, and helps resolve disputes involving brokers.

5.8.3 Indian Institute of Insurance Surveyors and Loss Assessors (III-SLA)

Founded in 2005, III-SLA is the professional body for surveyors and loss assessors. It certifies and trains professionals, sets ethical standards to keep loss assessment impartial, and works with IRDAI to maintain standards in claims assessment.

5.8.4 Insurance Information Bureau of India (IIB)

The IIB was set up by IRDAI in 2009 as the sector's central data repository, headquartered in Hyderabad. It collects and analyses data on premiums, claims, and underwriting across insurers, providing the evidence base that supports sound pricing, the detection of emerging risks, and informed regulation.

CHAPTER 6

Entities under the Ministry of Corporate Affairs, PFRDA, and Others

This final chapter brings together the bodies that govern companies, pensions, the resolution of bad debt, and workplace social security. At its centre is the Ministry of Corporate Affairs, which administers company law and oversees a cluster of regulators and tribunals; alongside it sit the pension regulator PFRDA, the asset reconstruction companies that clean up bank balance sheets, and the social-security organisations EPFO and ESIC.

6.1 Ministry of Corporate Affairs (MCA)

The Ministry of Corporate Affairs (MCA) is the Government department responsible for the regulation of companies and limited liability partnerships. It administers the Companies Act, 2013, the Limited Liability Partnership Act, 2008, and, with the Insolvency and Bankruptcy Code, 2016, the framework for corporate insolvency. Through these laws it governs how companies are formed, run, and wound up; it sets corporate-governance and disclosure standards, protects the interests of investors and creditors, and works to make doing business easier, including through the MCA21 electronic-filing portal. It carries out these functions through field offices and a set of specialised bodies and tribunals, profiled below.

6.2 Bodies under the Ministry of Corporate Affairs

6.2.1 Registrar of Companies (RoC)

The Registrar of Companies is the office, present in each state or union territory, that registers companies and LLPs and keeps the public record of them. It incorporates new entities, receives their annual returns and financial statements, processes changes to their constitutional documents, and acts against those that fail to comply, including by striking defaulters off the register. It is the front line of company-law administration.

6.2.2 Serious Fraud Investigation Office (SFIO)

The SFIO is the Government's specialist agency for investigating serious and complex corporate fraud. Set up in 2003 and given statutory standing under the Companies Act, 2013, it is a multi-disciplinary body that probes major financial irregularities, accounting fraud, and corporate misgovernance, and it can prosecute offenders. It works with other agencies such as the Reserve Bank, the Enforcement Directorate, and the Income Tax Department.

6.2.3 National Company Law Tribunal (NCLT)

The NCLT is the quasi-judicial body that adjudicates company-law disputes, mergers and amalgamations, oppression and mismanagement, winding up, and is also the adjudicating authority for corporate insolvency under the Insolvency and Bankruptcy Code, where it admits cases and approves resolution plans. It was constituted on 1 June 2016 and on the same day replaced the former Company Law Board.

6.2.4 National Company Law Appellate Tribunal (NCLAT)

The NCLAT, also constituted on 1 June 2016, hears appeals against the orders of the NCLT and of the Insolvency and Bankruptcy Board, and against certain orders of the Competition Commission. It is a key link in the chain of corporate adjudication, ensuring that decisions below it are sound in law, with further appeal lying to the Supreme Court.

6.2.5 Competition Commission of India (CCI)

The CCI is the regulator that promotes and protects competition in the market. Established under the Competition Act, 2002, and fully functional from 2009, it prohibits anti-competitive agreements such as cartels, checks the abuse of a dominant position, and reviews large mergers and acquisitions to ensure they do not harm competition. By keeping markets contestable it protects consumer welfare and supports innovation.

6.2.6 Insolvency and Bankruptcy Board of India (IBBI)

The IBBI is the regulator of the insolvency system, established on 1 October 2016 under the Insolvency and Bankruptcy Code, 2016. It regulates the professionals, professional agencies, and information utilities that make the resolution process work, frames the rules for insolvency and liquidation, and conducts research and training. Its purpose is the time-bound resolution of distressed firms, which both protects creditors and improves the flow of credit.

6.2.7 Investor Education and Protection Fund Authority (IEPFA)

The IEPFA, established in 2016 under the Companies Act, 2013, administers the Investor Education and Protection Fund, made up of unclaimed dividends, matured deposits, and similar amounts that companies must transfer to it after seven years. It refunds these amounts to rightful claimants and runs investor-awareness programmes. (This is distinct from the separate investor fund maintained by SEBI.)

6.2.8 National Financial Reporting Authority (NFRA)

The NFRA is the independent regulator of the auditing and accounting profession for larger companies, constituted in 2018 under the Companies Act, 2013. It monitors the quality of audits, sets and enforces auditing and accounting standards, and can take disciplinary action against auditors and audit firms for misconduct, strengthening the credibility of corporate financial statements after a series of audit failures prompted its creation.

6.2.9 Indian Institute of Corporate Affairs (IICA)

The IICA is the MCA's autonomous think-tank and capacity-building institute, established in 2008. It trains corporate professionals and government officers, including officers of the Indian Corporate Law Service, conducts policy research, and promotes good corporate governance and responsible business.

6.3 Professional Institutes

Three statutory institutes, all under the administrative control of the MCA, regulate the professions on which corporate compliance and reporting depend.

6.3.1 Institute of Chartered Accountants of India (ICAI)

The ICAI, established in 1949 under the Chartered Accountants Act, 1949, regulates and develops the profession of chartered accountancy. It sets accounting and auditing standards, conducts the CA examinations and training, enforces professional ethics and discipline, and advises the Government on accounting and taxation matters.

6.3.2 Institute of Company Secretaries of India (ICSI)

The ICSI regulates the profession of company secretaries, who are central to a company's legal and governance compliance. Granted statutory status under the Company Secretaries Act, 1980, it conducts the CS examinations and training, sets standards of professional conduct, and advises on corporate-governance and company-law matters.

6.3.3 Institute of Cost and Management Accountants of India (ICMAI)

The ICMAI, established in 1959 under the Cost and Works Accountants Act, 1959 (and formerly known as ICWAI), regulates the profession of cost and management accountancy. It sets cost-accounting standards, conducts the CMA examinations, and promotes cost control, budgeting, and performance management in business.

6.3.4 Other Professional and Management Bodies

Several other bodies serve the wider corporate and management ecosystem: the Institution of Valuers (1968) sets standards for the valuation of assets and businesses; the All India Management Association (1957) promotes management education and practice; and the Indian Institutes of Management, autonomous business schools under the Ministry of Education, train managers and conduct research that informs corporate practice.

6.4 Pension Fund Regulatory and Development Authority (PFRDA)

PFRDA is the statutory regulator of the pension sector. It first began work as an interim authority in 2003 and became a statutory body under the PFRDA Act, 2013, which took effect in 2014; it is headquartered in New Delhi. Its mandate is to regulate and develop the pension market and to protect the interests of subscribers, principally through the National Pension System and the Atal Pension Yojana.

6.4.1 Mandate and Functions

PFRDA registers and supervises the pension fund managers and other intermediaries that operate the system, lays down the investment guidelines they must follow, and monitors the performance and safety of subscribers' funds. It also promotes retirement awareness and financial literacy, develops new pension products, and works to extend pension coverage, part of the wider financial-inclusion effort, to the self-employed, informal-sector, and rural workforce.

6.4.2 National Pension System (NPS)

The NPS is PFRDA's flagship scheme, a voluntary, defined-contribution pension introduced in 2004 for new government employees and opened to all citizens in 2009. A subscriber contributes during working life into a non-withdrawable retirement account (Tier I), with the option of a flexible, withdrawable account (Tier II); the money is invested across equities, government bonds, and corporate debt by professional fund managers, and the subscriber can choose the asset mix. The scheme is low-cost and carries tax benefits, and on retirement it provides a mix of lump sum and annuity pension.

6.4.3 Atal Pension Yojana (APY)

The APY, launched in 2015, is aimed at workers in the unorganised sector who lack access to a formal pension. In return for small, regular contributions it guarantees a fixed monthly pension from the age of sixty, giving old-age security to those outside the organised workforce.

6.4.4 Recent Developments

Two recent additions have widened the system. NPS Vatsalya, launched in 2024, lets parents open and build a pension account for a minor child. The Unified Pension Scheme, operationalised from 2025, offers eligible central-government employees an assured pension as an option within the NPS framework.

6.5 Asset Reconstruction Companies (ARCs)

Asset Reconstruction Companies are specialised financial institutions that buy non-performing or distressed loans from banks and financial institutions, usually at a discount, and then work to recover value from them. By taking bad loans off banks' books, they let banks clean up their balance sheets and return to fresh lending. ARCs are regulated by the Reserve Bank of India and operate under the SARFAESI Act, 2002, which gives them powers to enforce security and recover dues.

6.5.1 How ARCs Operate

An ARC acquires a distressed asset and then seeks to resolve it, by restructuring the loan, negotiating a settlement, selling the underlying security, or enforcing it under the SARFAESI Act. To fund these purchases it issues Security Receipts to investors, which represent a claim on the recoveries from the underlying assets. The aim throughout is to maximise the value recovered from a loan that has already gone bad.

6.5.2 National Asset Reconstruction Company (NARCL)

NARCL is a Government-backed ARC set up in 2021 to tackle the largest non-performing assets in the banking system, typically those above ₹500 crore. Owned mainly by public-sector banks, it acquires large stressed accounts and pays banks partly in cash and partly in Security Receipts that carry a Government guarantee, which improves recovery certainty for the banks. Its resolution work is carried out with a paired entity, the India Debt Resolution Company Ltd (IDRCL), which manages and resolves the acquired assets.

6.5.3 Major ARCs and Industry Bodies

The first ARC, Asset Reconstruction Company (India) Ltd (ARCIL), was set up in 2002 by a consortium led by major banks; other significant players include Phoenix ARC, Reliance ARC, and Kotak Mahindra ARC. The Indian ARC Association represents the RBI-licensed ARCs before regulators and policymakers, while broader business chambers such as ASSOCHAM (1920), FICCI (1927), and CII (1895) provide wider forums in which the industry engages on policy.

6.6 Social Security Organisations

6.6.1 Employees' Provident Fund Organisation (EPFO)

The EPFO is one of the largest social-security bodies in the country, established in 1952 under the Employees' Provident Funds and Miscellaneous Provisions Act, 1952. It runs retirement savings and related benefits for organised-sector workers, administering the Provident Fund, the Employees' Pension Scheme, and the Employees' Deposit-Linked Insurance scheme, into which both employer and employee contribute. Most of its services are now available online.

6.6.2 Employees' State Insurance Corporation (ESIC)

The ESIC administers the country's contributory health and social-security scheme for organised-sector workers, established under the Employees' State Insurance Act, 1948. Through a network of hospitals and dispensaries it provides medical care to insured workers and their families, along with cash benefits during sickness, maternity, disablement, and, in the event of death, support for dependants.

Conclusion

This handbook introduces a range of regulatory authorities, financial institutions, and entities within India's financial system. The chapters provide concise information on each, offering an overview of the institutions and entities that form part of the country's financial framework.

Disclaimer

This handbook is intended to bring relevant content together in one place to support learning and understanding. Portions of the text were drafted with the assistance of generative AI tools for synthesis and formatting, under the author's supervision. The author has reviewed, edited, and verified the content and assumes full responsibility for its accuracy. If any discrepancies or errors are found, readers are encouraged to share feedback at vijaykiranslp@gmail.com. Suggestions and corrections are welcome.

www.ingramcontent.com/pod-product-compliance
Lightning Source LLC
Chambersburg PA
CBHW071358130726
47996CB00002B/988